DOCTRINE OF KARMA

DOCTRINE OF KARMA

A STUDY IN THE PHILOSOPHY AND PRACTICE WORK

SWAMI ABHEDANANDA

GYAN

Published by

Gyan Publishing House
5, Ansari Road
Daryaganj, New Delhi-110002
Phone: 011-47034999, 9811692060
E-mail: books@gyanbooks.com

Distribution Network
gyanbooks.com
India, USA, Canada, UK, Australia

ISBN: 978-93-7316-114-3 (PB)

First Published, 1944

2nd Impression 2025

Printed at: Gyan Press, Delhi.

DOCTRINE OF KARMA
Author: SWAMI ABHEDANANDA

DOCTRINE OF KARMA

A STUDY IN THE
PHILOSOPHY AND PRACTICE OF WORK

Hartsook
PHOTO

DOCTRINE OF KARMA

A STUDY IN THE

PHILOSOPHY AND PRACTICE OF WORK

By

SWAMI ABHEDANANDA

CALCUTTA

RAMAKRISHNA VEDANTA MATH

19-B, RAJA RAJKRISHNA STREET.

PREFACE TO THE NEW EDITION

The present volume contains Swâmi Abhedânanda's lectures on *Doctrine of Karma* and *Philosophy of Work,* delivered in America. In these illuminating lectures the Swâmi expounds the philosophy of work in that lucid and vigorous style which characterizes all his writings. The two pieces appended to the book were in the nature of two short lectures given by the Swâmi by way of a reply to questions which will help the readers in forming a clear idea of the subject. New references, detailed contents and an index have also been added for the convenience of the readers.

Râmakrishna Vedânta Math
19B, Râjâ Rajkrishna Street
Calcutta

The Publisher

DOCTRINE OF KARMA

CONTENTS

CHAPTER I

CHAMPER IV

CHAPTER V

CHAPTER VI

CHAPTER VII

APPENDIX A

APPENDIX B

न हि कश्चित् क्षणमपि जातु तिष्ठत्यकर्मकृत् ।
कार्यते ह्यवशः कर्म सर्वः प्रकृतिजैर्गुणैः ॥
तस्मादसक्तः सततं कार्यं कर्म समाचर ।
असक्तो ह्याचरन् कर्म परमाप्नोति पुरुषः ॥

No one can remain absolutely inactive even for a moment. Propelled by the power of nature, one is forced to work.
Therefore, do thou always perform actions which are obligatory, without attachment; by performing action without attachment, one attains to the highest.

—*Bhagavad Gitâ, Ch. III*, 5 & 19.

"The doctrine of Karma alone, can explain the mysterious problem of good and evil and reconcile man to the terrible and apparent injustice of life.

Any action that is not done through the attachment to the result of action, is for the purification of the soul, and as soon as the soul is purified the knowledge comes and the law of Karma ceases to exist. That is, the law of Karma is transcented. Thus one goes beyond that law. The Karma Yoga teaches that by performing all the obligatory works, without seeking any return for the individual, that is, through non-attachment, we gain the purification of the heart, and when the purification of the heart comes, it reflects the Divine wisdom, and that Divine wisdom kindles the fire of knowledge, which burns out all the Karma, good or bad, and the individual soul becomes absolutely free. That is the goal of the Karma Yoga."

Swâmi Abhedânanda

LAW OF CAUSATION

सर्वारम्भा हि दोषेण धूमेनाग्निरिवावृताः ।

Works are always followed by their defects and demerits just as the fire is enveloped with smokes.

–Bhagavad Gitâ, Ch. XVIII, 48.

DOCTRINE OF KARMA

CHAPTER I

LAW OF CAUSATION

A careful study of nature reveals to us that the phenomena of the world are linked together in the universal chain of cause and effect. No event can occur without having a definite cause behind it. Whatever we see, hear or perceive with our senses is but the effect of some cause whether known or unknown. To trace the causes of events and to become familiar with the conditions under which an effect is produced have always been the aim of the various branches of science and philosophy.

All science and all philosophies of the world unanimously declare that the law of cause and effect is the most universal of all laws. It is the one law which governs all phenomena however gross or fine they may be. All the forces of nature whether physical or mental obey this law and can never transcend it. From the vibrations of electrons to the revolution of the earth round the sun, from the falling of an apple on the ground to the raising of an arm by the will-power, every event is the effect of some invisible force working in harmony with the law of causation.

Similarly, every action of our body or mind is the result of some force or power which is its cause; but at the same time that which is the effect of some cause becomes in turn the cause of some grosser result, and that again produces some other still grosser effect, and that again a finer one, and so on and on the chain of cause and effect continues to spread without stopping anywhere, without coming to an absolute end. For instance, a murderer shoots the Austrian Archduke and drives a bullet into his body and the Archduke dies of blood-poisoning. Here, shooting is an action which is the effect of the mental and physical activities of the murderer. But the same action is again the cause of driving the bullet in the Archduke's body; this is the cause of the wound, which brings fever and other organic disorder, which results in his death. The death of the Archduke causes his wife to become a widow which produces changes in her life and in her whole family. The effect of this single act of murder did not stop here. It brought on the European war and caused destruction of life and property of millions and affected the whole world. It is needless to describe the horrors of the last war. The German Emperor lost his throne and empire. The Czar was assassinated. People are still reaping the effects of this war which will last for generations to come. Furthermore, it reacted upon the murderer, brought to him incalculable misery and untimely death. It left an impression upon his mind which he carried with him and perhaps his suffering will continue even after his death in another life.

Thus, we can see, how one event can be both a cause and an effect at the same time, and how it can affect the whole world producing various kinds of effects on the plane of the living as also on that of the dead. From this endless chain of cause and effect we can neither separate one single link nor call it useless or unnecessary. In the same manner, it can be shown that every action however minute or trivial it may appear to us, being conditioned by the universal law of causation, produces different effetcs visible and invisible and affects the whole world of phenomena either directly or indirectly. No action can escape this law, that every cause must be followed by an effect, that every action is bound to react upon the actor with similar force and effect.

This universal law of causation is called in Sanskrit the law of *Karma*. The word *Karma* is now almost naturalized into English. It comes from the root *Kri* to act and means action, or deed. Any action, physical or mental is called *Karma*; and as every action is bound to produce its re-action or result it is also *Karma*. Moreover, secondarily as an action is both a cause and an effect at the same time, the word *Karma* includes both the cause and the effect. In this universal sense, motion, attraction, gravitation, repulsion, moving, walking, talking, seeing, hearing, thinking, willing and desiring nay, all the actions of body, mind and senses are all *Karma*. They produce results being governed by the irresistible law of causation.

Under the sway of this all-pervading law of *Karma*, there is no room left for a chance or accident. What we call happening by chance or accidental is in reality the product of some definite causes which we may not know or cannot trace on account of our limited knowledge. The causes might be on the moral or spiritual planes, but we seek only on the physical plane. In ancient times when the range of the known causes was extremely limited, the uncultured people used to explain the accidental event or events produced by unknown causes, by attributing them to some supernatural powers or agencies. Even today there are many who believe in accidents. Gradually, when all the supernatural powers were unified into one personal God the effects of unknown causes were called Providential. But in reality all accidents have natural causes whether we know them or not. That which appears to be supernatural or Providential to an unscientific mind, is natural to a scientist or a philosopher whose conception of nature is larger and more universal. Therefore, all chance-events or socalled accidental occurrences are just as much governed by the law of causation or

Karma as any ordinary result of some known cause.

The results of the various causes of nature can be classified as *good, evil* and *mixed*. That which fulfils our interest and is beneficial to us under certain conditions is called *good;* and that which injures us in any way, is called *evil*. The *mixed* results are those which are partly beneficial or helpful and partly injurious. These three kinds of results determine the nature of actions or causes. If the result is good or, in other words, if we see any action producing an effect which is either beneficial to oneself or to one's neighbours physically, morally or spiritually without injuring any living creature mentally or physically or in any other manner, it is called *good;* while that action is *evil* which destroys the interest of oneself or of one's neighbours and brings suffering, sorrow, misery, to the individual worker or to other members of the society. The *mixed* results are those which serve the interest of some, bringing happiness to one or many, but at the same time they produce evil in some other quarters. In short, action which produce good at the expense of the interest or rights of others, are called the causes of *mixed* results.

In this world of relativity within the limitations of time and space, it is impossible to find any action which is absolutely good or which produces a result that creates no discord or disharmony in any shape or manner in any part of the world. **सर्वारम्भा हि दोषेण धूमेनाग्निरिवावृताः**[1] –Works are followed by their defects and demerits just as the fire is enveloped with smokes. It is impossible to find any work producing absolute evil effect, without causing some kind of good somewhere. Ordinarily, in judging a result when we see the preponderance of good over evil, we call it *good* and where evil predominates we say, that

1. *Bhagavad Gitā*, Chap. XVIII, 48.

action is *evil, wrong or sinful.* Wherever there is perfect harmony, peace, tranquility or happiness there is the result of *good* acts, and wherever discord, disease, suffering, pain, misery, injury, unhappiness prevail, there is to be found the violation of the laws of health, of life as well as of the moral laws, consequently, there is *evil.*

LAW OF ACTION AND REACTION

DOCTRINE OF KARMA

नादत्ते कस्यचित् पापं न चैव सुकृतं विभुः ।

God never rewards the virtuous nor punishes the wicked.

—Bhagavad Gitā, Ch. V, 15.

CHAPTER II

LAW OF ACTION AND REACTION

The law of causation or of *Karma* includes the law that the like produces the like, or that every action must be followed by a reaction of similar nature. If I strike a blow on the table, the table will react upon me with similar force. If I strike harder, I shall receive harder blow in return. As on the physical plane, so on the finer mental plane, all mental actions produce similar reactions. Motives, desires, thoughts and other mental functions being subject to the same law, produce *good, bad* or *mixed* results according to the nature of those mental activities. As all the mental activities determine the character of the individual ego, or the worker, we can easily classify the workers as *good, bad* or *mixed.*

The character of an individual is again

subject to the law of *Karma* because, it is the aggregate of a large number of minute activities of the mind-substance to which we give different names such as desires, tendencies, thoughts, ideas and impressions; everyone of which is governed by the law of action and reaction. Each character or personality is the grand total result of previous mental actions, and is also the cause of future changes in the character.

In the chain of cause and effect, it can be shown that each effect is latent in the cause and each cause is latent in the effect, applying the same law we can understand that every form of character is in itself a cause as well as an effect. The law of *Karma* inculcates this grand truth of nature, that cause lies in the effect and effect is also latent in the cause. For instance, a seed contains the whole tree potentially and produces the tree, and the tree produces the seed again. With the help of this great truth we can easily explain why a character is good or bad, or why one individual behaves in this way or that, or why one suffers and is miserable, while another enjoys his life and is happy. We do not have to blame our parents for our misery and sufferings. It is our own *Karma* that produces its results in the form of joy or sorrow, pleasure or pain, happiness or unhappiness. It is compensation. Every thing that we possess in this life, is the effect of our previous *Karma* or action, both mental and physical. Our present character is the resultant of our past and our future will be determined by our present acts. Neither God nor Satan is responsible for our pleasure and pain, happiness and misery. Thus, all the inequalities and diversities of characters can be scientifically explained by this law of *Karma.*

In the face of this universal law of *Karma,* there is no room for the hypothesis of predestination and grace which is accepted by the majority of orthodox Christians. The hypothesis of predestination and grace teaches that God, the Creator of all, settles the destiny of man before his birth. He preordains before the birth of each man and woman what he or she will be in future. The whim of the Creator makes one sinful or virtuous, before the time of one's birth. But this hypothesis destroys our moral responsibility and personal freedom. If we are all predestined by God to be sinful or virtuous, to be happy or unhappy, we can neither undo our destiny nor act against the Divine decree. It makes us absolute automata bound hand and foot by the chain of slavery. Furthermore, it makes God partial and unjust. Why should He make one innocent creature destined to suffer and another to enjoy? Why is it that one obtains His grace before one's birth and another does not? If a sinner be destined to sin even before his birth, why should he be responsible for his works, and why should he suffer for the whim of the omniscient and almighty Creator? If God be merciful to all of His creatures why should he not make all equally good and virtuous, moral and spiritual? These questions remain unanswered by the theory of predestination and grace. But they do not rise in the doctrine of *Karma*. If we can once understand that each individual soul reaps the results of its previous acts and deeds then we can never advocate the theory of predestination and grace. Every effect is measured by its cause.

A believer in the law of *Karma* is a free agent and is responsible for all the good and bad results of his own actions that attend to his life. He knows that he creates his own destiny, and moulds his character by his thoughts and deeds. He never blames another for the suffering and misery which come to him. He learns by experience the true causes of events and removing the bad or evil, he performs such actions which produce good to all as well as to himself.

He who obeys the law of *Karma* is more

moral and more virtuous than one who blindly obeys the Ten Commandments. He stands on a more rational ground than one who fears the punishment of God. He shrinks from doing any thing wrong, not because it is written in a book or scripture, but because he knows that every wrong action will sooner or later react upon himself and will make him unhappy and miserable. He performs good deeds for the reason that they will bring good reaction in the form of happiness, peace, tranquility and higher enlightenment. What we call rewards or punishments of God are nothing but the reactions of our own mental and physical actions. The doctrine of *Karma* denies the arbitrary Ruler and teaches that God never rewards the virtuous nor punishes the wicked-नादत्ते कस्यचित् पापं न चैव सुकृतं विभुः ।[1]

1. *Bhagavad Gitâ, Ch. V, 15.*

LAW OF COMPENSATION

DOCTRINE OF KARMA

न मां कर्माणि लिम्पन्ति न मे कर्मफले स्पृहा ।
इति मां योऽभिजानाति कर्मभिर्न स बध्यते ॥

Actions do not bind Me, nor have I any longing for the result of action. Whoever knows Me thus is not fettered by action.

—Bhagavad Gītā, Ch. IV, 14

CHAPTER III

LAW OF COMPENSATION

The doctrine of *Karma* includes the *law of compensation* and the *law of retri bution.* These are the fundamental verities of nature. As every effect must have a cause, every consequence must have an antecedent, so also there must be equal balance between a cause and its effect, between an antecedent and a consequence. A cause must always produce an effect of similar nature both in quality and quantity and a reaction must be similar to action. The forces of nature operate neither for profit nor for loss but for a perfect balance or harmony. If there be a surging of a high wave in the ocean there must be a deep hollow at its sides. If there be a flow of waters here, there must be an ebb somewhere. If there be tremendous heat in one place, extreme cold will be found in another place. When it is day here it is night in America. A long peace is followed by a long war, and *vice versa.* In this manner, we can show that polarity exists in every department of nature and brings in the end a perfect balance, equilibrium, harmony and justice; in short, it produces what we understand by the word *compensation.* The *law of compensation* is as irresistible as the law of causation and as relentless as the law of action and reaction. In fact, these three as well as the *law of retribution* work together. They represent merely the different phases of nature's purpose in producing diverse phenomena, each opposing the other. Take for an example H^2Q produces water. H^2Q is the cause, the antecedent, and water is the effect, the consequence. It is also the reaction and perfect compensation. There is neither increase nor decrease anywhere. A molecule of water contains two atoms of

Hydrogen and one atom of Oxygen, nothing more nor less. Similarly, heat is not only the effect and reaction but compensation for the fuel which produces it, nothing more nor less. Again electricity is the compensation for that energy which has been transformed into it. Electricity pays for energy and energy pays for it; there is neither debt nor profit anywhere but perfect balance.

As in the physical nature every force works for compensation so in the mental, intellectual, moral and spiritual planes the same *law of compensation* is manifesting itself with equal regularity. There cannot be bargaining in the realm of nature. What you wish to get, you must have to pay for it first, in thought, word and deed. Something cannot be obtained for nothing. In our daily life when we seek for a bargain either in buying or selling we forget this law and make many mistakes and suffer or repent in the end. A man goes to buy a collar but comes home with a refrigerator. He thinks that he has got a bargain. But he does not know that he has paid just what is its worth, nothing more nor less.

The *Law of compensation* exists not only for insentient matter and force but it also governs the sentient beings and intelligent souls. Whatever we suffer physically or mentally may appear to be unjust, may make us feel that we do not deserve it, but when we trace its cause and compare with it, we find that it is perfectly right and a just compensation. When we disconnect a headache from dissipation or indulgence of a previous night, it appears to be wrong, but connected with its antecedent it is just right and we deserve it. We cannot judge a thing correctly if we do not connect the effects with their antecedents. The causes determine the nature of the effect, the antecedents their consequences. If the cause be evil, the effects will bring evil return. No man can defy this *law of compensation.*

But the processes of this law in connection with the affairs of our lives are extremely intricate and they generally involve a cycle of beginning, growth and maturity. This cycle may take a short or a long period of time to complete itself. A man may reap the result of compensation for his works either in this life or after death in another incarnation, just as now we are reaping the results of the works of our previous lives. If we deny pre-existence and reincarnation of the soul and admit that the physical birth is the beginning of our life and by death ends all, then the chain of cause and sequence will be broken abruptly and the process of compensation will be unexpectedly interrupted by death. Then, there will be no compensation for the wicked who commit crimes and apparently enjoy all the blessings of life; nor for the virtuous who perform good unselfish works and do not get any return whatever during their life-time.

So long as we look upon our individual lives as isolated events beginning with the birth of the body and ending with its death, we shall not find correct explanation of anything but will see injustice and wrong at every step. But when we connect our present lives with our past, and our future, and standing upon the broad platform of eternal life that is, past and future life, if we look at our present we shall see justice and compensation at every step. Our present is the resultant of our past, and our future will be the resultant of our present thoughts and deeds. Suppose our life begins each morning and lasts for twentyfour hours. If we disconnect the life of today from the past of yesterday and of the future of tomorrow, and judge each day by its results, we shall find very poor compensation for our daily labour. Furthermore, it will seem terribly unjust to have our life falling on a wet and gloomy day with many accidents and unpleasant experiences, and another on the following day which is bright, sunshiny with many pleasant and happy experiences. Shall we be able to explain each of these fragments of life complete in itself? No. As our earthly life consists of a series of such daily lives so our eternal life of the soul consists of many periods of earthly lives. Earthly life when compared with the eternal soul-life will appear to be a mere fragment as small as a life ending in twenty-four hours. The compensation for the apparent physical suffering and misery of a good and virtuous man or woman during his or her earthly career is to be found in the soul-life. The blows on the body will by the *law of compensation* raise the soul of a truly spiritual person above the level of the ordinary mortals and such a soul will eventually command respect and honour of all nations in times to come. Conversely, the wicked and dishonest who apparently enjoy prosperity does so at the expense of their spiritual life and the compensation will be found in their soul-life. The *law of compensation* covers the whole chain of our individual lives. The broader the basis of reckoning there is, the more perfect is the compensation. Therefore, if we wish to see a perfect balance of causes and effects, of actions and reactions, we must take the widest view of the soul-life and reckoning from that standpoint we shall find satisfactory solution of all perplexing problems and most complicated affairs of human life.

LAW OF RETRIBUTION

DOCTRINE OF KARMA

रागद्वेषवियुक्तैस्तु विषयानिन्द्रियैश्चरन् ।
आत्मवश्यैर्विधेयात्मा प्रसादमधिगच्छति ॥

A wise man moves about among the objects of senses free from love and hatred keeping the tranquil state of mind absolutely controlled by his true Self.

—*Bhagavad Gitā, Ch. IV, 14*

CHAPTER IV

LAW OF RETRIBUTION

As every good act brings its own reward by the *law of compensation,* so every crime or wrong act brings its own punishment by the *law of retribution,* whether it is found in this life or in the next. When a robber robs another, he robs himself first. He who cheats another is in reality cheating himself. No one can do wrong without suffering evil effect in the end. Wicked act and its result or reaction which we call punishment grow on the same stem. The former is like the flower and the latter is the fruit.

The *law of retribution* is the inexorable necessity in nature. Every action reacts and brings its own reward or punishment first in the inner nature or soul, and then in the external circumstances in the form of gain or loss, prosperity or adversity, health or disease. The soul perceives the causal retribution, but the people call the change of external circumstances as retribution which comes after sometime. This law manifests itself in the soul long before the external changes appear. We have to pay the penalty for wrong doing, but not for good deeds. Virtue, wisdom, truth and love are real good; they proceed from God and therefore no one pays penalty for practising them. They are spiritual qualities; the more we practise them, the more they increase. He who seeks material good must pay taxes, but there is no tax on spiritual good.

The law of *Karma* teaches that the virtuous reward themselves and the sinners punish themselves by their own thoughts and deeds. Emerson says: "Every act rewards itself first in our own soul then in circumstance. People call the circumstance retribution."

St. Bernard said: "Nothing can work me damage except myself; the harm that I sustain, I carry about with me and never am a real sufferer but by my own fault." It is for this reason that the Hindus although do not believe in the hell-fire doctrine and do not fear the punishment of God, still they hesitate to commit wicked deeds and struggle hard to live virtuous lives simply fearing the eternal law of *Karma*. The Buddhists who do not believe in a personal God and who deny the existence of the permanent entity of the soul, have founded their ethics and religion upon this universal law of *Karma,* or of cause and sequence.

The doctrine of *Karma* is the fundamental principle of the philosophy and religion of Vedânta. But there is a difference between the Buddhistic and Vedântic interpretation of this doctrine. The Buddhists deny the existence of a soul entity as doer, performer of acts, thinker, enjoyer or sufferer. They say, that there is no duality of a doer and his doings, a thinker and his thoughts, an enjoyer and enjoyments. The words doer, thinker, enjoyer, sufferer are mere modes of speech. The realities of our soul-life, according to Buddhism, consist in doings, thoughts, sufferings, enjoyments and aspirations. These actions are called *Karma,* out of these a man is made, but he has no permanent soul. These *Karmas* constitute one's personality which is preserved beyond death. The Buddhists maintain that the eye sees, the ear hears, and thoughts think, that all mental and physical actions of an individual produce *Sanskâras* or subtle forms such as deed-forms, thought-forms etc., which continue to exist even after his death and reproduce similar actions through another body in future, being guided by the law of causation (*Karma*). Vedânta, on the contrary, admits the existence of a soul entity. The same intelligent and conscious self is called doer, thinker, enjoyer or sufferer. There is neither intelligence nor consciousness in the nature of physical or mental actions. As actions they are insentient. Vedânta refutes the Buddhistic interpretation by pointing out its fallacy that if there be no permanent soul entity the doer of an action or the sower of a seed will not be the reaper of its fruit. If there be no identity of the doer and the reaper, there will be a great confusion in the world of actions. It will be like one person eating the food and another getting the effect and not the eater, which is perfectly absurd. Moreover, it will be against the 'law of action and reaction' which teaches that all reaction comes back to the source from where the action started or proceeded. Otherwise, a sinner after committing sinful acts will reap the result of the virtuous deeds of another man. There is nothing to prevent this anomaly. Therefore, Vedânta says that the law of *Karma* necessitates the identity of the thinker or doer and enjoyer or sufferer. As this chain of *Karma* is beginningless and endless the soul entity which is the source of all thoughts and actions is therefore, beginningless and endless. It existed before the present birth. The results of the previous actions, each individual soul is reaping now and at the same time sowing the seeds of future results by performing good and bad deeds. The *Karma* that is stored is called *Samchita. Prârabdha Karma* is that which has been the cause of the present birth, body and character. *Kriyamâna Karma* is what we are sowing now; and *Agâmi Karma* are future actions. The same idea was conveyed by St. Paul when he wrote in the 6th Chapter of his epistle to the Galatins, (*verse 7th*): 'Whatsoever a man soweth, that shall he also reap.' 'And let us not be weary in well doing; for in due season we shall reap, if we faint not' (*verse*

9th). Perhaps, Christ also referred to the law of *Karma* when he answered the question of his disciples: 'Who did sin, this man or his parents that he was born blind?' Jesus answered: 'Neither hath this man sinned nor his parents.' Of course a man who was born blind could not sin in that incarnation and when it was not the result of his parent's sin, where was the cause of his blindness? Heredity cannot explain it. The theologians say, it was the will of God because they believe in the theory of predestination which as I have already said makes God partial and unjust. The only rational explanation that can be found is through the doctrine of *Karma,* that is, the previous actions of the same man were the cause of his blindness. Applying the law of *Karma,* Vedânta will explain that he was reaping the result of his evil action which he did in his previous incarnation. There cannot be any other satisfactory and scientific explanation of such cases. Thus, if the law of *Karma* is so universal as to govern all phenomena of the world as well as of our thoughts and deeds, if it is so inexorable as to make every individual soul reap the results of actions either in this life or in the next, and if it be true that every reaction, being similar in nature as the action itself, is bound to return to the centre of action or in other words, to react upon the actor making him or her happy or miserable, how important it is for every one of us to remember this law at every moment of our life; and how necessary it is for every one of us to be extremely cautious in performing the duties of daily life so that we shall not sow the seeds which will bear unpleasant and disagreeable fruit and which will make us unhappy and miserable either in this life or hereafter.

The doctrine of *Karma* alone, can explain the mysterious problem of good and evil and reconcile man to the terrible and apparent injustice of life. Those who believe in this noble doctrine are never disturbed in their minds at the sight of the inequalities of birth and fortune or of intellect and capacities around them. The knowledge of this universal truth prevents them from cursing life or human beings or from blaming their supposed Creator when they see fools and profligates are honoured in society, when they find their neighbours possessing neither intellect nor any of the noble virtues are prosperous and enjoying all the comforts and pleasures of life on account of their births in wealthy families. The doctrine of *Karma* tells us the reason why people suffer although they might not have done any wrong in this life, although they apparently seem not to deserve any kind of suffering. It is the *law of compensation.* The law of *Karma* eternal as it is, predestines nothing and no one; but on the contrary, making every one free agent for action, shows the way out of the world of misery, through good thoughts and good deeds. *Karma* creates nothing, nor does it plan or design anything. We create by our actions the causes of good and evil and receive reward or punishment as the reactions of our thoughts and deeds by the *law of compensation.* The poor and suffering classes will find no consolation anywhere but in this one doctrine of *Karma.* It is for this reason, there is so much of contentment among the poverty-stricken people of India who can hardly earn enough to keep their body and soul together. If this noble doctrine be preached among the innumerable discontented and wretched people in Christendom, they would find a ray of hope for their future, they would try to live better lives, they would be more moral, more virtuous and more spiritual than they are today. They would be able to bear the burden of misery upon their shoulders with more calmness, with more patience, contentment and peace.

PHILOSOPHY OF KARMA

DOCTRINE OF KARMA

किं कर्म किमकर्मेति कवयोऽप्यत्र मोहिताः ।
तत्ते कर्म प्रवक्ष्यामि यज्ज्ञात्वा मोक्ष्यसेऽशुभात् ॥

Even wise men are deluded on this point, what is action and what is inaction. I shall tell thee the philosophy of work, by knowing which thou shalt attain to absolute freedom from all imperfections.

—*Bhagavad Gitā*, Ch. IV, 16.

CHAPTER V

PHILOSOPHY OF KARMA

Those who understand the philosophy of *Karma* and act accordingly, are pure in heart and enter into the life of Blessedness.

In Sanskrit this philosophy of work is called *Karma Yoga*. It is one of the methods by which the final goal of Truth may be realized. There are three others: that of love, that of wisdom, and that of concentration and meditation; but all these paths are like so many rivers which ultimately flow into the ocean of Truth, and each is suited to the mental and physical conditions of different individuals. One in whom the feeling of worship is predominant will naturally choose the path of love and devotion; another, more philosophical, will take that of discrimination; a third will prefer the practice of concentration and meditation; while those who have an instinctive tendency to work, who are neither philosophical nor able to concentrate or meditate, and who find it difficult to believe in a personal God, may, without worship or devotion, reach realization through the knowledge of the secret of right action.

Karma Yoga means literally 'skill or dexterity in work', and it deals with all activity whether of body or mind. Recognizing that activity is an inevitable condition of life, that no human being can live without performing some kind of work, either mental or physical, it seeks through its teaching to show how this constant output of energy may be utilized to acquire the greatest spiritual enlightenment and to attain to perfection and absolute freedom. This can be accomplished as we are told in the fourth chapter of the *Bhagavad Gitâ*, by seeing in the midst of activity that which is beyond all action. "He who sees activity in inaction as well as that which is above all action in the midst of the activities of mind, body, and senses, is wise among mankind, is a true *Karma Yogî,* and a perfect doer of all actions."[1]

Ordinarily we identify ourselves with the work that we are doing, and being driven on by the relentless necessity to act, we make ourselves like machines, labouring without cessation until at last we grow weary, discouraged, and unhappy. When, however, we realize that there is within us something which transcends all activity, which is unchanging, immovable, and eternally at rest, then we accomplish our daily tasks without discouragement or loss of strength, because we have learned the philosophy of work.

There are five conditions necessary for the accomplishment of all mental or physical labour. First, we must have a physical body,

1. कर्मण्यकर्म यः पश्येदकर्माणि च कर्म यः।
स बुद्धिमान् मनुष्येषु स युक्तः कृत्स्नकर्मकृत् ॥
—*Bhagavad Gitâ, Ch. IV,* 18.

for it is the storehouse of energy. If we are without a body, we can do nothing on the physical plane. This body, furthermore, must be in good condition. If there is disease of any kind, it is unfit for right work. Second, there must be present the sense of the *Ego* as the doer or actor. We must be conscious of the '*I*' who feels the impulse to work and proceeds to follow that impulse. Third, we must have the instruments with which to work; these are many: there are the sense organs—the eyes, ears, nose, tongue, and sense of touch; the five instruments of physical work—the hands, feet, etc.; and the internal instrument, the brain or mind-substaince, with all its faculties—the power of will, cogitation, determination, memory. Fourth, we must have the desire or motive to work; and fifth, there must be some sort of environment. Without this last, senses, external instruments, and brain would avail us little. To hear a sound with our ears we must have the air; to see, there must be light and a medium to transmit its waves; while the body cannot move without space. These five conditions are essential to every kind of work, whether good or bad; and in the practice of *Karma Yoga* we must be perpetually mindful of them, never confounding one with the other, but holding ever before us the body, its instruments, and the knower or self-conscious actor as distinct one from the other.

The results of actions performed under these five conditions are of three kinds: those that are desirable because they help us to fulfil our aims in life, and bring us comfort and pleasure; second, those which are not desirable; and third, those which are partly desirable and partly undesirable. It is not possible to escape some one of these results at every moment of our existence; since, as has already been said, the activity of our organism never ceases. Practically speaking, there cannot be absolute rest of body or mind. Even when the body seems at rest, the mind substance continues in a state of vibration; and when here, again, all conscious activity apparently stops, as in the case of deep sleep, subconscious activity still goes on in the organic actions of the system, such as unconscious cerebration, digestion, breathing, circulation; for we are learning through the investigations of science that the unconscious mind extends over a much larger area than the conscious mind; also that all conscious activity first rises there. Each of these activities of mind, furthermore, is bound to produce some kind of result.

If, therefore, activity is inevitable and each action must produce its result, what can we do to make all such results harmonize with the highest ideal of life? By searching for that which, in the midst of our varied activities of mind and body, remains always inactive. When we have found that and recognized it, we have understood the purpose of the philosophy of work, and can make our every effort lead us to the final goal of all religion, to the relization of Truth, and to the attainment of Blessedness. If we cannot do this, we shall be forced to go on reaping the fruit of our actions and continue in the suffering and misery which we now endure. By practising the teachings of the philosophy of work, on the other hand, we shall not only bring freedom to the soul, but shall rise above all law and live on a plane above motion. From the minutest atom up to the grossest material form, there is constant motion. Nowhere is there rest. One thing, however, moves not; one thing is at rest, and *Karma Yoga* explains what that is, how we may realize it and make ourselves one with it.

That something which is beyond all activity is called in Sanskrit *Atman*. It is the Knower in us. If we use a higher discrimination and try to understand the nature of the Knower, by observing our internal processes while we are doing anything, we shall discover that the Knower is constant. The reader knows that he is sitting and also that he is reading. In other words, he distinguishes two distinct objects of knowledge; but the consciousness with which he perceives them, remains the same. In like manner, the Knower of all these different activities of mind and body is always identical. When we hear a sound, we know that we hear; when we see a light we know that we see; but is the knower of sight different from knower of sound? No. That which knows the object of sight or the object of sound is always the same; it does not change. It was the same ten years ago and will be the same tomorrow. The Knower of all the experiences of our childhood is just the same as the one who knows what we are doing now. If we study and realize this, we shall find that the Knower is unchangeable and not bound by the conditions which govern the changeable. If it were otherwise, and if changeable and unchangeable were subject to the same conditions, not only would it be contrary to the established order of things, but must cause great confusion, since there would be no way of differentiating changeable from unchangeable.

That which is subject to time, space, and causation is changeable; while that which is beyond these is unchangeable. Time, for instance, means *succession,* which is a condition of thought; and space means *co-existence.* The activities of mind, being either in succession or simultaneous, produce the ideas of time and space; they are conditions, or, as Kant calls them, 'forms of thought.' One thought following another gives us a conception of intervals which we call *time;* while, when two ideas rise simultaneously, that which separates them is what we call *space.* Thus, that which exists between the idea 'me' and the idea 'sun' we classify as space; yet it is purely a mental concept, having no existence outside the mind; for who knows any concrete thing designated space? Hence, since these ideas of time and space are merely conditions of thought, they must be subject to change, because our thought is continually changing. Any thing which takes form in the mind and is conditioned by time and space must change; but the Knower, not being a condition of mind or limited by time and space, does not change. A certain thought rises in our minds and passes, then another takes its place, to be followed again by still another; yet the witness or Knower of all these thoughts, whether of gross objects or of abstract ideas, remains the same. The Knower, when identified with the changes of the mind, becomes knower and thinker. Thinking is an activity of the mind substance; it is a vibratory condition of this substance; and when the Knower takes upon itself that condition, it becomes knower and thinker. When it identifies itself with sense powers, and sense perceptions, it becomes knower and perceiver; and it becomes the conscious mover or the physical man when it is one with the conditions and activities of the body.

In this way, if we analyse our mental activities and study the nature of the Knower, we find that it is the permanent source of intelligence, above mind and beyond thought, that it is in reality neither thinker nor actor. The *Atman* or Knower can have neither desires nor passions, for they are purely mental conditions. When the Knower is identified with any mental activity, we feel, it is true, that we have desires and passions, but in reality we are only the Knower of desire. When we are angry, the mind is put into a certain state of vibration which is unpleasant. At first we perceive that anger is rising in us; then gradually, as it gains strength, it covers the whole mental plane and reflects on the Knower. Lacking the power to separate ourselves from the mental condition, we become identified with the wave of anger and we say: 'I am angry.' At the outset we saw anger as a state of mind, but by degrees it becomes inseparable from the Knower in us until at last we imagine ourselves one with it. In this manner, when the Knower comes to be identified with the conditions of the mind, of the organs of work, and of the body, we appear to be doers and seek the results of our work.

When we are identified with the body, we feel pleasant and unpleasant sensations in the body. Environmental changes produce certain effects upon our system and we fancy that we are one with these effects, and that they cause us pain and suffering; but in reality these changes do not affect the Knower of sensation. If, for instance, the weather changes, there will be a corresponding change in the physical organism; yet if we can separate ourselves from the body, it may experience such a change without our feeling it. If we can learn this lesson of dissociating the Knower from all changes of body and mind, and never confounding our mental and physical conditions with the immutable Being within us, we have made a great stride towards realizing the ideal of the philosophy of work.

To accomplish any work there must be present knowledge, the object of knowledge and the Knower. For instance, before we can go from one place to another, we must be conscious of the act of going; such knowledge is indispensable, and the object of knowledge—that is, where we are going—is equally necessary, while neither can exist without the Knower. Knowledge, again, is of three kinds. First, the knowledge of the thing or of the sense object, not as it is in reality but as it appears to us. We have the five objects of knowledge: sound, colour, odour, savour, and touch. These we can perceive with our five senses and through these channels we acquire this first stage of knowledge. We learn that things exist around us, but such knowledge being limited, we do not arrive at an understanding of these things as they really are. We say ordinarily, for example, that we hear a sound or see a colour, locating sound and colour outside of us. If, however, we analyse the nature of sound or of colour, we find that sound is nothing but vibration of air carried by the auditory nerves to the brain where we perceive the sensation, which when projected outside, becomes external sound. Similarly it can be shown that the colour we see is not in the object or in the luminous rays which emanate from the object, but is caused by ether waves in a certain degree of vibration. That vibrant ether coming in contact with retina and optic nerve, produces a kind of nervous stimulation which results in the sensation of colour in the brain. By projecting these sensations outside of our bodies we locate them on distant objects and then say that we see this or that colour.

Again, if we are going to some place, we may think that we are walking toward the north at the rate of two miles an hour; but our knowledge of this fact is only relatively correct, for to estimate our speed accurately, we must know all the conditions which affect our walking. How can we say that we are moving northward at a speed of two miles an hour, when we know that the earth is rotating on its axis from west to east at the rate of twenty-five thousand miles in twenty-four hours, or over one thousand miles an hour? Again, it is whirling round the sun at the rate of eighteen miles per second, or sixty-four thousand eight hundred miles per hour; while the sun and the whole planetary system are travelling with a tremendous velocity in a grand, far-sweeping spiral motion around some other centre. Such being the facts, how imperfect is the knowledge which makes us think that we are moving towards the north. In reality there is neither north nor south. From our standpoint we may seem to be walking at the rate of two miles an hour, but our speed will be increased a thousandfold in another direction when we take into consideration the diurnal motion of the earth and its annual revolution round the sun. Furthermore, it can be shown that from the standpoint of the universe we are not moving at all. Since the whole universe is in reality a unit, where will it move? It cannot move anywhere. Therefore as a part of it we are not moving and can go nowhere. Thus by proper analysis we have been carried from the first to the second kind of knowledge—from the limited knowledge of the conditions under which the body seems to be moving, to the higher knowledge of the conditions as they actually are, and not as they merely appear to be. From this we may pass to the third or highest kind of knowledge, which reveals to us the unity of existence. With the help of this knowledge we learn to look at things from the standpoint of one absolute Reality which is the eternal Knower of the universe. The moment that we think that our body is a part of the universal body, our mind not separate from the cosmic mind, and that our souls, being parts of one universal Soul, are most intimately connected with one another, all activity assumes a new meaning for us, and it becomes impossible for us to act from selfish motives or to do wrong. It is when, on account of our imperfect knowledge, we identify our true Self, the Knower, with the limitations of mind and body, that we become selfish and are ready to do the things which bring us suffering and misery. If, however, we remain conscious of the oneness of the universe, of the laws that govern mind and body, of the relation which one soul bears to another, and of the various planes existing in the universe, we cannot make any mistake whatever. The light of true knowledge dispels the darkness of ignorance which is the cause of selfishness, and reveals the true nature of the Knower which is above all activity.

That knowledge is the highest which brings us into conscious harmony with the universe, which makes us realize that the Knower is separate from the object known, and that nothing in the universe can ever exist without depending upon the existence of one universal Knower, which manifests through each individual form. This highest knowledge of oneness kills the idea of separateness and resolves the multiplicity of phenomenal objects into that underlying Reality which is one. The phenomenal objects of the universe, such as sun, moon and stars, are in truth like so many eddies in the vast ocean of matter in motion. Apparently they are separate from one another, but they are closely connected each with the other by the undercurrent of that primordial energy, which manifests itself as the various forces of nature. The sum total of this energy in the universe is neither increased nor diminished, but is eternally one. It is also inseparable from the infinite

Being, which is the source of existence and consciousness. Being deluded by appearances, we get the idea of separateness and see one body as distinct from another; but when we go below the surface and seek that which produces variety, tracing it back to its final cause, the eternal energy, we inevitably arrive at the knowledge of oneness. This is the problem which every individual will have to solve. It has been solved already thousands of times by the best thinkers and philosophers of the world, but their solution cannot bring satisfaction to others. If one person has realized the oneness of existence, he will possess true wisdom, freedom from all delusions, and unbounded peace of mind; another, however, cannot gain the same result until he has risen to a like relization. With the attainment of this highest knowledge of oneness all questions will be answered, all doubts will cease; but it is impossible to make the unawakened mind grasp what this means, for to understand, one must have experienced it for himself.

The first kind of knowledge, as has been already said, is the most limited. It is the knowledge of the fleeting appearance of sense objects as reality. Animals know their food, they hear sound, they smell, taste, and feel the changes of the weather; but that is all. They do not understand the causes of their sensations; their mind does not function on a plane higher than that of the senses, hence they know nothing of the things imperceptible to the senses. Those who are living on this plane of sense perceptions are like animals. They do not believe in the existence of things which cannot be revealed by the senses; they cannot differentiate matter from spirit, soul from body, or the knower from the object known; consequently they always identify themselves with their mental and physical activities. The majority of people in every country have not as yet advanced beyond this first stage of knowledge; and it is for this reason that they are so narrow in their ideas, so selfish, so intent on seeking the comforts of the body and the pleasures of the senses without thought of others. Many are still even below the higher animals in the matter of faithfulness, devotion, and care of their young.

Such knowledge, however, is in reality ignorance; and the philosophy of work strives to lead us out of this state of darkness to that of the highest enlightenment, by which we may recognize the true relation of the individual to the universe, and ultimately realize the goal of unity. Ordinary people are as unconscious of this oneness as they are of the fact that they are carrying a weight of fifteen pounds to every square inch of the surface of their bodies. Think what a total weight this means! So great, indeed, that if the body were put into a vacuum, where this atmospheric pressure would be no longer exerted, it would immediately burst. Yet people bear this burden day after day without knowing it until they try to climb some steep ascent. So it is with the knowledge of their true nature. Having no realization of it, they believe that they have learnt everything, because they have learnt to care for the body; but the wise man laughs at such primitive conceptions of life. At every step we meet this ordinary knowledge, which is based on some particular idea, narrow and limited in scope, with no element of higher knowledge in it; and it is this ignorance which is the cause of all of our mistakes. To avoid them, we must continually ask the question: Who is doing the work? Spirit, mind, senses, or body? Who is the worker? If we wish to put the philosophy of work in practice, we must keep this thought constantly in mind. Then we should next ask: What special work must we do to attain to the realization of the Knower?

First of all, we must train our minds. We

must open our eyes to the conditions under which we work; and when we have learnt to distinguish between the knower and the actor, we shall find it easy to apply this knowledge to our everyday life. We must remember that the five conditions already described are absolutely necessary for any kind of work; but they can in no way influence or affect the Knower. Intellect, mind, body, and senses exist in relation to it and cannot be active if cut off from it; but they are perpetually changing, while it is unchangeable. He who realizes this—that all things on the mental or physical plane exist only so long as they are in relation to the *Atman*, the absolute source of life and knowledge, sees that one which is inactive in the midst of all activity, and becomes a right worker. Such an one attains to perfection through his work.

Let the body work, then, while we remember that it is the mind and the sense organs which are working, and that we are in reality the Knower, the *Atman*. Anything else is not permanently connected with us. We have taken this body for the time being and are using it for the fulfilment of the highest purpose of life; but through ignorance of the fact that our true Self is above all physical conditions, we have identified ourselves with our material instrument. Not realizing that we transcend all activity, we have imagined ourselves one with our mental modifications and our organic functions; and having fettered ourselves with desires, we are struggling to satisfy them. When, however, we recognize that these desires are not permanently related to the true Self, that they exist in mind only, and that we can use them as a means of attaining to perfect freedom, then they will cease to bind us and we shall find rest and peace in the midst of our troubles. If anger or hatred or desire surge up within us, we have only to separate ourselves from that mental change and it will vanish. If passion arise, we have only to

remember that we are the witness-like Knower of passion and it will subside. It is when we forget that we are the Knower, and become identified with anger, passion, or hatred, that we fall under their dominion.
By studying the conditions under which we perform all work, we can separate our true Self from those conditions and be happy. Then we work without considering results; but the moment that we think of gaining some specific end, we delude ourselves and work ignorantly, for the knowledge possessed at that time is partial and imperfect. Perfect knowledge reveals the Knower which is above all activities and the reality which underlies all phenomenal objects; understanding this, we live in the world and labour, without being enslaved, like ordinary workers, by desire for work or for its results. To the outsider we may appear to be like other workers, but our mental attitude is different; and though we may outwardly resemble them, we are not, as they are,

affected by the tasks which we perform with our body, mind, and senses; nor are we prompted by selfish motives.

Wise men work ceaselessly, being conscious at the same time that they are not working, allowing the body and mind to act, but seeking nothing in return. According to the philosophy of work, all those, moreover, who do not assert the self, who are free from attachment, endued with energy and perseverance, unaffected by success and failure, and who constantly do their work unmoved by desire for or aversion to the fruits of their actions, are, like these wise ones, true spiritual workers. Those, on the other hand, who are passionate, ambitious, easily affected by joy or grief, gain or loss, are ordinary workers of the world. They are never happy, but are always disturbed, anxious, and uneasy. Beneath these is still a third class of workers, the lowest of all. It includes those who are heedless, foolish, arrogant, dishonest, indolent, procrastinating, and depressed in spirit; who act without regard to the loss or injury which they may inflict upon others; and who are ever ready to deprive their fellow-beings of their rights or prevent them from gaining their livelihood. Such workers are looked upon as criminally selfish, as well as wicked; yet all their wickedness, selfishness, attachment, and passion proceed only from ignorance of their true Self, who is the unattached, witness-like Knower of all things, and who remains unchangeable in the midst of the changes of mind and body.

Such is the fundamental principle of the philosophy of work, and those who comprehend it, understand that which made all the great spiritual workers of the world declare: 'I am one with the eternal Truth,' or as the Hindu philosophers express it: *'I am Brahman, I am He, I am He.'* They who keep this idea constantly before the spiritual eye, will obtain undounded happness in this life; and when change comes to the body, they will not perceive it, so intense will be their realization of the fact that they are above all change. Such persons have learnt the secret of work. They are peaceful, blessed, and the true workers of this earth.

SECRET OF KARMA

DOCTRINE OF KARMA.

कर्मण्येवाधिकारस्ते मा फलेषु कदाचन।
मा कर्मफलहेतुर्भूर्मा ते सङ्गोऽस्त्वकर्मणि ॥

To work thou hast the right, but never to the fruits. Be not actuated by thirst for the results of action, nor be thou pleased in inaction.

—Bhagavad Gitâ, Ch. II, 47.

CHAPTER VI

SECRET OF KARMA

This world may be compared to a gigantic stage, where the drama of life is constantly going on. Individual souls are the actors; they play the parts for which they are best fitted, their desires, tendencies, and capacities determining their acts. One takes the part of a president, of a king, a governor, or prince; another, that of a merchant or lawyer; a third, that of a husband; a fourth, that of a mother; but each without exception plays his rôle day after day and night after night, contributing, either consciously or unconsciously, to the vast drama called life, with its various acts and scenes, some tragic, some serio-comic, some melodramatic. The large majority of mankind, however, do not realize that they are thus acting on the stage of the world. They have forgotten that they, themselves, have selected the rôles which they are impersonating, that by their own choice they have assumed these characters. They fancy, on the contrary, that some invisible being has forced them to fill these parts; and whenever they achieve a gratifying result, they imagine that that unseen being is pleased; while, if the result be painful, they weep and wail and blame the same invisible power.

Occasionally some of the actors or actresses, disliking their own parts, try to change with others whose parts seem more attractive, because they show a little merriment in their play; so they pass from one rôle to another. Always, however, they continue to act on this world stage, gaining experience at every step, as they move onward toward the fulfilment of the purpose of the drama. This purpose is the emancipation of the soul from slavery to the laws of nature and from the bondage of ignorance, selfishness, ambition, and all imperfections which hold it down on the plane of phenomena. Those who attain the goal retire from the stage and appear no more. They live in bliss and happiness in the higher realm of Divinity.

The cause of all these different parts which the individual souls are playing, lies within the actors and actresses themselves and not outside of them. In their own inner nature is it to be found; and as the power of growth, which is latent in the seed buried beneath the surface of the earth, gradually bursts forth and manifests itself in the form of plants, trees, and shrubs, each showing the peculiarities contained in the original seed, so these powers that are slumbering in each human soul, wake up in time, stir it to action, and force it to assume some particular part in the play. It is these latent powers when roused to activity that we know as our desires and motives. So long as these desires and motives are perfectly dormant, there is no sign of activity; and this latent or dormant state is called in

Sanskrit *Tamas*. We can understand its character better if we examine the condition of deep sleep. In that state the power of walking, of hearing, speaking, is latent and finds no outward expression. It is a state of inertia or inactivity; but when this power wakes up, it produces a vibration in the mind substance, and this vibration we call mental activity. This again, when manifested on the external plane, appears in the form of physical activity. All physical activity, however, necessarily presupposes mental activity.

Each germ of life possesses infinite potentialities stored up within it; and these, as they pass from the condition of *Tamas* to that of active desire, drive it on through the various stages of evolution—from the vegetable into the animal kingdom and on to that of man. The first glimmering of mental activity appears in the lower animals; and it reaches its climax when the germ of life manifests as a human being. In the human form the mind attains its highest state of activity, and this active state of mind is called in Sanskrit *Rajas,* the meaning of which is activity. This impels the individual to express itself in mental and physical action, which produce certain impressions on the mind, and these impressions become the seed of future activities and desires. Thus every action, whether physical or mental, has three states: First, activity or desire; second, outward action; third, impression. After this it remains dormant for a time, then wakes up, appears in the form of desire, expresses itself in some action, of mind or body, and again produces an impression.

Each individual is bound by these three conditions: activity or desire, work, and impression. We cannot arrest our external work so long as there is mental activity. We are impelled to some kind of exertion by our own inner nature. For this reason it is said in the *Bhagavad Gitâ.*

"None verily, even for an instant, ever

remains doing no action; for every one is driven helpless to action by the energies born of nature." Unable, therefore, to resist this inner force, we are bound to do that which we are doing. Each of our actions, furthermore, must inevitably produce some result. Every action is followed by a corresponding reaction, which returns to the point from which it started; hence the reaction of each action must come back to the soul itself and influence the doer. Further study also shows us that the character of action and reaction must be the same. If the action be good, the reaction will be good; if the action be evil, the reaction will likewise be evil. This 'law of action and reaction,' or of cause and effect, is called in Sanskrit *Karma*. Bound by this law of *Karma*, each individual soul is performing

1. न हि कश्चित् क्षणमपि जातु तिष्ठत्यकर्मकृत् ।
कार्यते ह्यवशः कर्म सर्वः प्रकृतिजैर्गुणैः ॥
—*Bhagavad Gitâ, Ch. III, 5.*

various works; each actor is playing his part and reaping its results, which are in the form of good or evil, happiness or suffering.

That which we are doing today is the result of the dormant powers with which we were born; and the cause of these powers lies in the activity of some previous state of existence. We have not received any of these latent powers from outside; but as we see that every action here leaves a certain impression which, after a period of quiescence, is again aroused, so the cause of existing desires must be found in impressions created by past action. Our present life is a connecting link in the chain of our appearances on the phenomenal plane. *Our present is the result of our past, and our future must be the result of our present.* Since this is true, then we can determine our past by studying our present. Many people ask: What proof is there that we have had a past and that we shall have a future? The proof is our present condition. And this can be demonstrated scientifically by the 'law of cause and sequence.' The cause is inherent in the effect, and the effect is the outward manifestation of the cause; therefore, if we are the effects of something, that cause must be, not outside, but within us. This we learn by observing nature and understanding the 'law of causation.' This law, moreover, is irresistible and relentless. It does not stop for the orphan's cry or for the widow's tears; it sweeps on without pity and unchecked by any obstacle. It moulds the character of every individual, of sages and sinners, of kings and beggars; every one is bound by it, no one can escape it. Driven by it, we are moving hither and thither, apparently in a straight line, but more often in a circle. Starting from one desire, we go to a certain distance, describe a curve, and come back to the same place without the smallest knowledge of where and how the purpose of life will be achieved.

In this wheel of action and reaction each individual soul is passing from one point to another, on and on, age after age. Is their any hope of extricating ourselves from this wheel? Ignorant and short-sighted people deny the existence of the law of *Karma*. They say that all activity will end after the death of this body; that nothing will remain; that no one will be responsible for this body's actions. But is it likely that the law of cause and effect, of action and reaction, will cease to function because these ignorant people do not understand and believe it? No. Whether we believe it or not, it will continue to produce its results, just as the law of gravity operates, whether a man observes or disregards it. Our belief or disbelief can never arrest the law of *Karma* in its ceaseless action.

Such being the decree of nature, and the consistency of the law, the questions arise: How shall we work, what shall we do to fulfil the purpose of this drama of life?

How can we free ourselves from this law which has made us slaves of desire and passion? These questions do not present themselves often to Western minds, because they do not realize their importance so strongly as the Hindus; and because they do not find in their religion any specific mention of the law of *Karma*. It is modern science that is bringing out into such strong relief this 'law of causation;' but the scriptures deal little with it. They try to explain everything by the law of heredity, or by the intervention of some supernatural power, always placing the cause of our deeds outside of us. They say that we are impelled by some external power to do certain things, but who or what that power is, they cannot tell us. In India, however, volumes upon volumes have been written on the subject; it has been discussed for ages; the law of *Karma* has been applied to the problems of everyday existence, and through it has come an understanding of the mysteries of life which has brought consolation to millions.

Since the law of *Karma* is so inexorable, every individual must be subject to it—not only in this life but also in future lives. Can there be then no escape from it? Will there not come a time when the soul will gain freedom from this bondage of nature? As a matter of fact, the soul is not created for nature, but nature is working for the experience of each individual soul. We must realize this; but until we understand the soul in its true light, we cannot discern whether physical nature was made for it or whether it was made for physical nature. If, however, we study our own souls carefully, we find that our mind, intellect, senses, and body are within the realm of phenomena; while the real Self is something which stands as a witness outside and beyond mind, intellect, body, and senses. That witness-like something within us is beyond nature and its laws. It is already free; if it were not, we should not seek freedom. The yearning for freedom is within us; and as there cannot be a yearning for something which does not exist in reality, we can safely say that there is such a thing as absolute freedom, *which will be attained sooner or later* as the ultimate purpose of every human life.

We have seen that all the causes of our actions are the motives or desires which lie within ourselves. So long as these desires are there, we are forced to work and reap the fruit of our labours. In everyday life each individual is constantly performing some kind of work from some motive. Some work for money, some for name and fame; some work in the hope of attaining heavens, and others as a penance. A certain number acquire immense wealth through their labours, and imagine that by the accumulation of riches they are fulfilling the purpose of life; but if this were true, these people would be perfectly happy and contented.

Yet when their storehouses are full, they still reach out for the peace and happiness which their wealth connot bring them. Such motives all proceed from selfishness; and so long as we foster them, we must reap the results of our desires, remain attached to them, and continue to be fettered by the chain of cause and effect. All work *done through selfish motives binds the soul to the fruits thereof, and is in consequence a cause of bondage.* If, however, we can once reach the point of working without having desire for results, without seeking any return, then the law of *Karma* will be broken and freedom will be ours. How can we do this? *By working for work's sake and not to fulfil selfish desires.*

Here it may be asked whether it is possible to work for work's sake. Of course, those who are striving for individual ends, such as name, fame, or money, will say that it is impossible; but there are a few in every country who work without personal motive, without desire for return, and they are the salt of the earth. They work as if they were paying off a debt which they owe to society, to parents, to humanity. If we can labour with this idea, that all we do is merely to cancel our debt to the universe, then we can work for work's sake. When we pay off a debt, do we think of getting something in return? No; we do our work, cancel our obligation, and think no more about it. Every individual, on account of his birth, owes something to state and country, to family and neighbours; to his spiritual teachers, and to his higher Self. While he lives in society, he owes a duty to society. So long as he is guarded and protected by social conditions, he is in debt to the social body which maintains them. How can he pay that debt? By being a good member of society, by doing what he can to help all other members, and by making every effort to fulfil his obligation to the community and to mankind. We must recognize the rights of others and not perform any act which may infringe upon those rights. We must not injure our neighbour, since we do not wish to be injured by him; and at the same time we must remember that our motive in working is not to get some return, but to pay off the debt which we owe to the world. By being good members of the family, and by bringing up our children in the right way, we pay our debt to parents and forefathers. By studying the works of great men and by learning all the wisdom which has been gathered by the wise ones, we cancel our debt to them; while we daily pay our debt to our spiritual teachers by following their example and precepts, and by helping mankind in the path of spiritual progress

In India every individual life is divided into four periods, each of which is fixed for paying off debts to some portion of the world —to parents, society, spiritual teachers, or to our own higher Self. The debt which we owe to this higher Self, can be paid by realizing our true nature, by knowing who and what we are in reality, and by emancipating the soul from the bondage of nature as well as from the irresistible law of *Karma,* which keeps it on the phenamenal plane. This debt should be cancelled before the time of departure comes, and in India this conviction is very strong. The ultimate aim of life will be served if we can discharge the debt which we owe to our own selves. If we keep this idea ever in our minds as we work in the family, in society, in the state, we shall work without seeking any result, whether personal glory, wealth, or even moral satisfaction; and all work performed in this spirit will purify our souls from selfishness, hatred, jealousy, and anger. Then we shall go to our round of daily tasks, eating, drinking, talking, not with the motive of preserving our bodies, but of creating the conditions necessary for the cancelling of all our debts. We shall no longer work through attachment to the fruits of our labour, and shall, in consequence, play our parts without reaping the results of sorrow, suffering, and disappointment, which too often come when the motive of our effort is a selfish one. Then also shall we be in no danger of wrong doing.

Another thing must be considered before we can work for work's sake. All the forces which we are using in our minds and bodies do not really belong to us. We claim them as our own, but in reality they are not ours. Can we say that the air in our lungs is ours? No; we are only making use of it for a certain purpose. Neither is the force of attraction which holds the molecules of our bodies together ours; it is in the universe. So when we understand our entire organism, physical and mental, we find that all the forces which we are using, belong not to any particular person, but to the universe. Looking at ourselves from the standpoint of the universe, we perceive that our bodies are like so many whirlpools in the sea of matter, every particle ot which is in constant motion. Similarly, when we realize the nature of our minds, we discover that there is one mental current flowing through the universe. When that current, which is known as the cosmic mind, appears in one form, I call it my mind, in another form you call it your mind; but in reality, it is acting in every mind. The one universal energy is manifesting through numberless forms and shapes and can never be regarded as possessed by any individual. The power of thinking, of hearing, tasting, smelling, all exist in the universe. Every force operating through the machinery of the human body is a force of nature; but being self-deluded, we dream that these forces are ours. Therefore it is said: "Actions are wrought in all cases by the energies of nature. He whose mind is deluded by egoism thinks, *'I am the doer.'*"[1]

1. प्रकृतेः क्रियमाणानि गुणैः कर्माणि सर्वशः ।
अहङ्कारविमूढात्मा कर्ताहमिति मन्यते ॥

—Bhagavad Gitâ, Ch. III, 27.

Foolish and self-blinded men fancy that they are the doers of their actions, and consequently continue to reap the fruits of their error throughout their lives. So long as we identify ourselves with our bodies, through ignorance of our true nature, and call ourselves actors, players, or doers, we must endure the results of our actions. The moment, however, that we realize that this body is a part of the universal body, that this intellect is a part of the cosmic intellect, that the knower of the mind, the senses, and body is not any one of these, but stands outside, and that this knower is our true Self; then we let the body work with the full consciousness that we are neither actor, worker, nor doer, and we remain untouched by the consequences of our actions. The one essential thing is never to forget that the work done by mind and body is in reality *not performed by the true Self, but by nature.* The wise ones realize this and are freed from the *attachments which proceed from ignorance.*

Selfishness is the result of ignorance. When we confound our true Self or *Atman* with the mind and body, we imagine that we are the narrow limited being whom we call *'I'* or *'Me,'* and refuse to recognize other limited beings known as *'He'* or *'She.'* We think of our own 'little self,' struggle to enrich that, and suffer from the results of our ignorance. By acting thus from selfish motives year after year, we make ourselves unhappy and miserable. The wise ones, however, comprehending that these different minds and egos are only expressions of the one cosmic mind and one cosmic ego, never make this mistake, but have regard to the rights of all, love others as they love themselves, and are therefore always happy. Whatever they do, is done not in ignorance but with knowledge. When they play their parts on the stage of this world, they are fully aware how the drama will end and how its purpose will be fulfilled. They work incessantly, never seeking results; for they remember the teaching of the blessed Lord Krishna: "To work thou hast the right but not to the results thereof."[1]

How can we expect to get the fruits of work done by nature, and not by ourselves? We cannot. By realizing, however, whence come the forces that are expressing through our minds and bodies, and by letting the results of their manifestations go to the source from which the activity proceeded, we shall cut ourselves loose from the chain of cause and sequence; and when that chain is broken we shall be free. Then we can let our hands and feet, our bodies and intellects, remain constantly active, without thinking of results or forgetting that we are not in reality the actors.

Some people imagine that by giving up action they will escape the law of *Karma;* but they are mistaken. Those who have read the

1. कर्मण्येवाधिकारस्ते मा फलेषु कदाचन ।

—*Bhagavad Gitâ, Ch. II, 47.*

Bhagavad Gitâ, will recall the passage where Krishna says to Arjuna, when, overcome with compassion, he refuses to fight his adversary: "Be not a coward, this does not befit thee; abandon this mean weakness of heart and arise, O conqueror of thy enemies![1] And again: 'Imbued with egoism (sense of *'I am the doer'*), thou art determined not to perform that to which thy nature impels thee. Constrained by thy nature-born activities, thou shalt be forced to do that which from delusion thou wishest not to do."[2]

This may be applied to our everyday lives. We cannot withdraw from the work of the world without, like Arjuna, being guilty of

1. क्लैब्यं मा स्म गमः पार्थ नैतत्त्वय्युपपद्यते ।
क्षुद्रं हृदयदौर्बल्यं त्यक्त्वोत्तिष्ठ परन्तप ॥
—*Bhagavad Gitâ, Ch. II,* 3.

2. यदहङ्कारमाश्रित्य न योत्स्य इति मन्यसे ।
मिथ्यैष व्यवसायस्ते प्रकृतिस्त्वां नियोक्ष्यति ॥
—*Bhagabad Gitâ, Ch. XVIII,* 59.

cowardice. Besides, however eager we may be to retire from a life of action, we cannot in reality pass outside the region of activity. If we cease to work with our bodies, our minds still remain active; and our only hope of freedom is in learning the secret of work. This consists, as we have already seen, in working ceaselessly without desire for return, and without other motive than the emancipation of the soul by paying our debts. He who can thus act is free from all the laws which bind the ordinary individual. His whole work is for mankind. All that he does is a free offering to the world. He has no interest in results; yet he works tirelessly, and through his labours his mind and heart become purified. Then on the mirror of his pure heart reflects the divine Spirit dwelling within him; and he feels that his mind and body are merely the instruments through which the Divine will is manifesting its power. Of such an one the *Bhagavad Gitâ* tells us:

"Having abandoned attachment for the fruits of action, ever content, dependent on none, though engaged in actions, nothing at all does he do."[1]

Liberated from the bondage of ignorance, selfishness, and delusion, and having cut asunder the thread which binds the soul to birth and rebirth, he attains at last to the realm of eternal peace. This peace is considered as the highest ideal by every religion, and with its realization the aim of life is achieved. Having reached this condition, the soul regains its perfect freedom. Being no longer subject to the laws of nature, it is master, and can manifest those powers of omnipotence and omniscience, which are its birthright. They who have attained to this state are called 'the Saviours of the world.' Such were Buddha,

1. त्यक्त्वा कर्मफलासङ्गं नित्यतृप्तो निराश्रयः ।
कर्मण्यभिप्रवृत्तोऽपि नैव किञ्चित् करोति सः ॥

—*Bhagabad Gitâ, Ch. IV,* 20.

Krishna, Christ, Râmakrishna, and others. Realizing the oneness of the individual soul with the universal Spirit, *they worked for work's sake, without thought of return,* and whoever will work in like manner, will know true happiness in this life and will remain in peace forever.

DUTY OR MOTIVE IN KARMA

वुद्धियुक्तो जहातीह उभे सुकृतदुष्कृते ।

He who performs his duty, understanding the secret of work, rises above good and evil.

—Bhagavad Gitâ, Ch. II, 50.

CHAPTER VII

DUTY OR MOTIVE IN KARMA

Activity of mind and body is the condition of life; absolute inactivity means death. This activity finds expression variously in the ordinary work of our everyday existence; and this work can be divided into three classes, according to the motive which inspires it.

The first class includes all that we do for the preservation of the body and for the gratification of the senses. The second embraces all actions done from a sense of duty; and the third, all that is done freely and with love. The actions of the first class, performed to satisfy the cravings of the animal nature, are mainly guided by two motives—hunger and propagation of species. If we go down into the vegetable kingdom, we find these motives expressed in the activity of trees and plants. From the lowest amœba to human beings the same expression is equally present, *the difference being not in kind but in degree.* As we rise higher in the scale of evolution, we observe that these motives become more clearly defined, until they reach their culminating point in man, the highest of all living creatures. Through a further process of evolution, these two motives again, when inspired by a love of self, produce the sense of right and wrong and the sense of duty. The second gradually develops from the first, and this invariably proceeds from love of self. This love of self, moreover, is very limited at the outset; since the self at this period is that which is identified with the body. Not only is this the case in lower animals, but in human beings also, who live on the animal plane and whose spiritual eyes are not open, and who identify soul with body and spirit with matter. They are unable to distinguish one from the other.

In every individual, at this point, the self is the centre of all things, and that which benefits the self becomes the unique object of attention; then the individual begins to call that which is beneficial to himself right, and that which causes him pain and suffering wrong. Moved by the love of self, he first takes care of the lower or narrow, limited ego, of that which we understand by the terms *'I'* and *'Me,'* without recognizing the 'Self' of others. At this stage of development he has no other thought than to seek his own pleasure and gratification, or to avoid that which may bring him discomfort and suffering; as we find in savage tribes, whose sole concern is for the lower self, who are, so to speak, all *'I,'* all *'Me.'* By degrees, when the moral nature begins to unfold, this same individual learns to reverence the rights of others; and by others here is meant those who are closely related to the self—the nearest relatives or those with whom the person is constantly associated. He now feels that he should not do anything to injure his nearest of kin; and this is the first dawning of the sense of duty. Henceforth, the idea of right and wrong is no longer confined to the motives of self-preservation and self-gratification, but includes the selves of those joined to him by family ties. When the individual finds a relative who cares for his bodily needs or gives him certain pleasures, he commences to feel for that relative, and thinks that he ought to protect his life and seek his comfort as he would his own. This is the awakening of the sense of duty towards the family.

Next, if he comes in contact with a neighbour who brings comfort or pleasure into his life, he develops for him the same feeling as that which he bears towards his blood relation, and he strives in turn to defend his interests. Hence the origin of duty towards friend and neighbour.

In this way, if in our own experience we try to trace the relation existing between us and those not connected with us by ties of blood, we shall find that our feeling of duty towards them has gradually sprung from the basic principle of love of self. The particular duty of individuals, however, will vary according to the nature and circumstances of each one; for *there can be no absolute standard of duty for all, since duty is in its essence relative.* In this great workshop of nature every one is bound to discharge the duties laid upon him by his special environments, and these environments are not always the same. As the environment varies, so will the duties vary; and as individual natures differ, so must the sense of duty differ, according to each nature and its specific tendencies. That which is duty for one person may not be duty for another; that which is duty at one period of life may not be such at another period. A child has its duties towards its parents, but when he reaches youth new duties arise. When he goes to school, he must assume the duties of the student life; when he marries, the duties of the married life begin; and when he becomes a father, duties to his children bind him. When, again, he remembers that he bears a definite relation to his country or state, he awakens to a sense of duty towards the nation and the government.

So, in the case of every individual, it will be found that what was duty at one moment ceases to be such at another; while new duties come up to take the place of the old ones. We all had certain duties at school, but where are they now? Gone! We do not think at present in the same way as we did when we were students; other duties have arisen and crowded out those of that time. Life is divided into different stages, and each stage has its obligations. It is a continuous process of evolution and progression, in which higher duties are evolving out of lower ones and binding the soul for the time being. When we go to our office, official duties claim us; when we return home, we are met by household duties. Our whole existence is a series of occupations, each of which brings with it a feeling of *ought;* and this feeling is the sense of duty in us. *There is no such thing as duty in an objective sense;* we cannot get it from outside. It is purely subjective. When we perform certain acts under certain circumstances, and are conscious that we ought to do them, that feeling of obligation is duty. But who tells us that we should? Our own inner self. Impelled by natural tendencies and partial knowledge, we begin to think that under specific conditions we should perform these acts; and so long as we hold to this belief, we are forced to do them. *The feeling which binds us to these special acts of body and mind is the sense of duty. Duty creates a kind of bondage* between the individual and his environment. If we do not have the sense of duty, we do not feel this bondage. It is, in fact, a condition which makes us slaves while it lasts. In our daily lives we discharge our many duties like bond-servants; yet we keep imagining that in doing them, we shall be happy through the satisfaction which will arise from the consciousness of having done them; but the next instant conditions change, our environment shifts, and we are confronted by another set of duties and a new feeling of *ought.*

Nothing can make us free so long as we are fettered by this sense of duty. *It is the greatest bondage of our lives.* We may look upon it as eminently commendable to be perpetually constrained by the idea of *ought* and to force ourselves to do that which seems to us duty for the moment; but it is absolutely necessary for us to realize that *this will never lead to happiness.* We have only to go back in our own experience to find that although we have performed numberless duties, we have not gained any lasting happiness from their accomplishment. If we should ask an old man of eighty or ninety, who has fulfilled all his obligations to family, society, and country, if he is happy, will his answer be in the affirmative? No; he will almost surely say: 'Although I have done all that was required of me as father, husband, and citizen, yet am I not happy.' Then we stop and put the question each to himself: 'If I do my whole duty, shall I be any more at peace?' And we are forced to admit: 'Most probably not.' The mere fulfilment of duty in itself cannot be productive of permanently good results. We must know, among the multiplicity of duties that surround us, which is the most important; and finally we must face the problem: 'What is the highest, the one real duty of life?'

Some people say that helping others is the highest duty. But why should we help others? Because some one has said so, or because it is written in some book? Why should we not kill everybody and enrich ourselves? The Bible declares: 'Fear God and keep His commandments, for this is the whole duty of man.'[1] The Qurân says: 'Follow the teachings of Mohammed; this is the whole duty of man.' Zoroaster tells us: 'Follow the teachings of the Zend-Avesta and obey the commands of Ahura Mazda; in this lies the whole duty of man.' But why should we fear God? The answer comes: 'Because if we do not, He will punish us.' But why does He command in one way for one nation and in a different way for another? How, when the scriptures all vary, can each lay claim to supreme authority? In the Qurân we read that a man may marry twenty times—Mohammed himself had eighteen wives—and this is one of the commands of God under the social conditions prevailing in that particular country; but it would scarcely do in America. Variation, indeed, is a salient feature of

1. *Eccles. Ch. xii., v.* 13.

socalled divine commands, and when a man has read all the scriptures of the world, he does not know which to follow. Why, then, should we obey the decrees of God? There are many who do not believe in punishment; what is left for them? They will not be impelled to observe God's commands, since they have no fear of His wrath; therefore such persons will have no duty.

The word *duty* is an abstract term, and, like all abstract terms, it cannot be defined. We can, however, get some idea of what is meant by it if we study the different scriptures and reduce their teachings to their simplest forms. In the commands of God, we observe that all those which say: 'Do not do this or that,' may be summed up in the admonition: 'Do not be selfish, be unselfish.' Let any divine command be analyzed, and this will be found to be its basis. Any action that leads one from selfishness to unselfishness, that broadens and elevates the character, that brings freedom to the soul and directs it Godward, is good, and therefore becomes the highest duty of every individual. On the other hand, that which shuts one within the narrow walls of one's limited lower nature, is selfish and should be avoided. When a man has realized this, his idea of duty will no longer be confined to the sayings of any book or of any person, but will be founded upon the universal law of unselfishness. His standard will be: 'That which uplifts the character is right, that which degrades is wrong.' The particular line of action, however, which will elevate or degrade an individual will vary according to his nature and his environment. Elevation and degradation should not be measured by the standard of any one particular person in one particular stage of development, but by the loftiest ideal of all individuals, of all sects, and of all religions. The highest common standard is the absolute freedom of the soul from every bondage. That which leads to such freedom is elevating, that which keeps one in bondage is degrading. Therefore it is said by Hindu philosophers: 'That which elevates the soul, which brings prosperity and absolute freedom, both here and hereafter, is true duty.' This ideal of duty is like the pole-star which points the way to the ship of the human soul in the troubled waters of the ocean of activity, gradually guiding it across the deep sea to the land of perfect freedom.

We have only to be constantly mindful of this one fact, that to be unselfish is our sole duty, and apply it to our daily round, to be sure that our highest duty is being accomplished. In ordinary life we are confronted by various kinds of duties—towards ourselves, towards our family, our neighbour, towards society, country, humanity, and finally, as the culmination, towards all living creatures; for the one idea which is universal and common to all in every country and in all ages is the non-injuring, either mentally or physically, of any living being. First we start from the lower self, from the *'I'* or *'Me,'* then by degrees we come to recognize the self of others. When we begin to feel for others in the same way as we do for ourselves, we commence to rise above the limitations of this narrow self; and at that very moment we have taken our first step towards unselfishness. The end is reached when we realize that all living creatures are equal to ourselves. Jesus the Christ said: 'Love thy neighbour as thyself,' and 'Love your enemies;' but He did not preach: 'Love all living creatures,' as did Buddha. When a goat was going to be killed, Buddha came forward and offered his own life for that of the goat. The goat's life was saved, and the man who would have killed it, afterwards became Buddha's disciple. When we begin to cherish all living creatures as we cherish ourselves, we have reached the state of development where the sense of *'I,' 'Me,'* and *'Mine,'* vanishes; where we see all creation as one on the spiritual plane. Therefore it is said in the *Bhagavad Gitâ*: "He who sees the same divine Self equally abiding in all, doth not kill himself by his Self and so attaineth the supreme goal."[1] This realization of oneness of spirit is the highest ideal of life. It is the climax of unselfishness, and becomes identical with Divine love, because God loves all creatures equally. His love, indeed, shines alike upon all, as does the light of the sun upon man and beast without distinction of kind.

When this love or feeling of oneness awakens in the soul, we rise above all duty, and work, not through a sense of obligation, but through love. Which is the higher of these two motives? Love must be higher than duty, and where there is love, there can be

1. समं पश्यन् हि सर्वत्र समवस्थितमीश्वरम् ।
न हिनस्त्यात्मनात्मानं ततो याति परां गतिम् ॥

—*Bhagavad Gitâ, Ch. XIII,* 29.

no thought of duty. We observe in ordinary life how, when one person falls in love with another, he loses all feeling of duty towards friends, relatives, and society; because love has annihilated all consciousness of other duties and freed the soul. *While we are bound by duty, we are slaves;* but if in this condition of slavery we are carried away by a strong feeling of love, all the sense of duty to family or society, which previously held us in bondage, melts away, and at that moment we become free. So we see that wherever there is true love, there is freedom, and no vestige of duty can remain. God has no duty towards any living creature, but He has love for all. We should try, then, to distinguish between love and duty; since duty puts us in bondage, makes us slaves; while love brings freedom and emancipation to the soul.

When the feeling of love towards every living creature comes to any one, that person is free from all duties, from all bondage, from all attachment to his physical nature. He does not seek sense pleasure, neither does he care to preserve the lower self nor to protect the body, because he realizes that he is not the body but soul. Even when the body is torn in pieces, he is not moved, but holds to the consciousness of his spiritual nature, his *Atman* or divine Self, which cannot be cut in pieces, cannot be burnt by fire, moistened by water or dried by air.[1] In realizing this, he also works without thought of return. Even those who do their duty with the hope of return, cease to think of results when they begin to be actuated by love; and *all work performed through this higher motive of love takes the form of acts of worship of the supreme Spirit.*

1. नैनं छिन्दन्ति शस्त्राणि नैनं दहति पावकः।
न चैनं क्लेदयन्त्यापो न शोषयति मारुतः॥
अच्छेद्योऽयमदाह्योऽयमक्लेद्योऽशोष्य एव च।

—*Bhagavad Gitâ, Ch. II,* 23-24.

Duty is seldom sweet when not accompanied by love; on the contrary, it is exceedingly bitter. Suppose a wife has to perform her duty towards her husband, if there is no love, is it pleasant? Or, if the husband must do his duty towards his wife, not from love, but simply because they are bound together by law, is there any happiness in it? Where there is love, however, there is joy and peace, and neither seeks any return.[1] True love makes one work for love's sake, and the sense of duty disappears. He who understands this, knows the philosophy of work; and, moved in all his actions by love alone, he becomes blessed and a divine worker.

Jesus gave himself to mankind because he loved them. Buddha helped humanity because he saw men miserable and suffering and could not resist his desire to save them,

1. युक्तः कर्मफलं त्यक्त्वा शान्तिमाप्नोति नैष्ठिकीम् ।
अयुक्तः कामकारेण फले सक्तो निबध्यते ॥

—Bhagavad Gitâ, Ch. V, 12.

any more than could a man who, seeing some one drowning and losing all thought of himself, of his very life even, rushes to the rescue. *That which makes us forget our own self or our own life is true love and beyond duty.* Or rather it is the fulfilment of the highest duty, and must therefore bring freedom. Then whatever we do, we do through love and live in this world like incarnations of Divinity.

The final end of duty is freedom and Divine love, and with the awakening of this love comes all knowledge. Divine love and Divine wisdom are one. They unfold the inner self simultaneously and lead us to God-consciousness. The moment that a man loves all living creatures as he loves himself, he has known the Self of all and has risen to the realm of Godconsciousness; he is no longer on the human plane. *Divine love means expression of the feeling of oneness.* This oneness does not appear on the physical but only on the highest spiritual plane; therefore when any one reaches this state, he knows God and sees Divinity in every thing. He does not see black man, white man, or lower animals, *but the divine Self behind these various forms.* God is manifesting everywhere and through every form equally.[1] When such a man looks on the face of a person, his eye-sight goes below the surface to bottom, to the very core, to the Soul of that soul; and through this deeper vision he perceives that the source of consciousness, existence, and bliss within that individual is the same as *Atman* or the Divine spark within himself. In thus seeing oneness, he performs his highest duty, becomes one with God, and declares as did Jesus the Christ: 'I and my Father are one.' He dwells in that supreme Godconsciousness for ever; he

1. सर्वभूतस्थमात्मानं सर्वभूतानि चात्मनि ।
ईक्षते योगयुक्तात्मा सर्वत्र समदर्शनः ॥

—*Bhagavad Gitâ, Ch. VI, 29.*

has no trouble, anxiety, or sorrow; he is free, emancipated and blissful.[1] How can there be any sorrow, suffering, misery, or pain where there is nothing but Divinity? All these exist where the idea of duality or multiplicity prevails; but with the recognition of spiritual unity comes the cessation of pain, sorrow, and suffering.[2]

The universe is one ocean of Divinity, and all fear of death and punishment must vanish with the realization of this Truth. The real Self never suffers. It is already divine and free from birth and death;[3] and when we

1. समदुःखसुखं धीरं सोऽमृतत्वाय कल्पते ।
—*Bhagavad Gitâ, Ch. II,* 15.

2. यत्र हि द्वैतमिव भवति तदितर इतरं जिघ्रति, तदितर इतरं पश्यति * * ; यत्र वा अस्य सर्वमात्मैवाभूत्तत्केन कं जिघ्रेत्, तत् केन कं पश्येत् (बृह० उ० 2. 4. 14.). अस्यैतदाप्तकाममात्मकाममकामं रूपं शोकान्तरम् (बृह० उ० 4. 3. 21).

3. न जायते म्रियते वा कदाचिन्नायं भूत्वाऽभविता वा न भूयः ।
अजो नित्यः शाश्वतोऽयं पुराणो न हन्यते हन्यमाने शरीरे ॥
—*Bhagavad Gitâ, Ch. II,* 20.

know this, life becomes worth living here and now. Otherwise, we may perform duties forever without finding peace and happiness; but when we realize our oneness with Divinity and reach that state of superconsciousness, or Godconsciousness, all our desires and duties are fulfilled, all the knots of our hearts are rent asunder, all doubts cease forever, all questions are answered,[4] and the individual soul passes all laws. He who has understood the one supreme duty and fulfilled that, has reached freedom and gained Divine love and Divine wisdom on this earth. He transcends all the law of *Karma*, the law of compensation and of retribution, and enters into the abode of everlasting existence, intelligence and bliss.

4. भिद्यते हृदयग्रन्थिश्छिद्यन्ते सर्वसंशयाः ।
क्षीयन्ते चास्य कर्माणि तस्मिन् दृष्टे परावरे ॥

—*Mundaka Upanishad*, 2.2.8.

APPENDIX

DOCTRINE OF KARMA

APPENDIX A

DELUSION

If all that we see and sense are delusions, what is the Truth? We have to understand the meaning of the word *delusion*. Delusion does not mean 'non-existence.' It means *relative reality,* that is, it exists for the time being, and has no permanent existence. Very few people know the meaning of delusion. They think that it is just like the mirage. You cannot realize that as a mirage so long as you are in it. I should say it is more like a dream. Dreams are real so long as we are dreaming, but when we wake up they become unreal. If all these things that we are doing be transitory, that is, exist for the time being, and we consider them as real, it is the same thing as if we are dreaming. But there is an awakening from this state of dream, and that is called 'superconsciousness.' It is Godconsciousness. Then it appears like a dream, but not at present. At present they are all real, and we must go on doing just as we are doing.[1]

We cannot find the Truth here under these conditions, but the Truth is behind all these appearances. It is the background. From the Truth we have come into existence, in the Truth we live, and into the Truth we return at the time of dissolution. The whole universe is pervaded by Truth, but we do not see it.[2] We see only *the appearance of Truth.*

1. सर्वव्यवहाराणामेव प्राग्ब्रह्मात्मताविज्ञानात् सत्यत्वोपपत्तेः । स्वप्नव्यवहारस्येव प्राक्प्रबोधात् । यावद्धि न सत्यात्मैकत्वप्रतिपत्तिस्तावत् प्रमाणप्रमेयफललक्षणेषु विकारेष्वनृतत्वबुद्धिर्न कस्यचिदुपपद्यते । * * तस्मात् प्राग्ब्रह्मात्मताप्रतिबोधादुपपन्नः सर्वो लौकिको वैदिकश्च व्यवहारः ।

—*Sankara Vâsyam,* 2. 1. 14.

2. यः सर्वेषु भूतेषु तिष्ठन् सर्वेभ्यो भूतेभ्योऽन्तरः, यं सर्वाणि भूतानि न विदुः, यस्य सर्वाणि भूतानि शरीरम्, यः सर्वाणि भूतान्यन्तरो यमयति, एष त आत्मान्तर्याम्यमृतः ।

—*Brihadâranyaka Upanishad,* 3, 7, 17.

Take, for example, a table. The table cannot remain for ever. If you burn it, it is gone. Where does it go? What remains then? If our body is destroyed, what remains then? We do not see it. So, from the unmanifested we have come into manifestation. We can perceive with our five senses. We can see, hear, smell, taste and touch. But what we see we do not know. You see colour, for instance. You see a beautiful colour in a flower. If you analyze it and study carefully, physiology will tell you that you do not see any colour there. There is no colour. There is some kind of vibration of ether. It is a play of light, and light is nothing but vibration. But an ignorant person says: 'I see it, here it is; how can I deny it?' It is true that he cannot deny it. But what he sees and feels is not just exactly what it is in reality. There is a certain kind of vibration which comes from the flower and produces a kind of inverted image on our retina. And that image even we do not see, but that image produces a molecular change in the optic nerve and in the cortex of the brain at the back of our head, and then it is translated into feeling or sensation. Then we try to trace the cause of that sensation, and by the law of causation we see it is there. That flower has caused this sensation, and we call it red or yellow or whatever colour you may call it. The colour could not exist if you did not have the optic nerve, the retina and the brain. It is a conditional existence, and that is the meaning of delusion. The real vibration we could not see or perceive with the senses, but it is there just the same. You may call it X. So, the real table, the foundation, the noumenon of this table, we do not see. We see only the colour, the form. Then we have the sensation of thinness or thickness, or roughness or smoothness. These are the qualities. But real substance we do not see. And therefore these qualities are the appearances. The substance is the permanent reality.

In the same way, there is a permanent reality in each one of us, but only our appearances of qualities which make up our personality are seen, and that personality is constantly changing. You are not the same person of the past when you were a boy or a girl. But you do not take into consideration all these changes. You think you are the same person, although you have a new body and brain. You are creating the brain anew all the time, and the nervous system. The whole organism has gone through a complete change, but still you are the same person. What is not changing there? What is unchangeable in you? That which is unchangeable in you has given the foundation of that identity that makes you feel that you are the same person. But you do not know that thing at present. That is the most important thing, but yet we do not know it. We are deluded that we are the same person, we are going to live here for ever, and this is our home. That is a kind of delusion we have. *It is a false knowledge* (*mithyâ-pratyaya*). It is indiscrimination. It is what is called 'undifferentiated consciousness'. And that is the meaning of delusion.

But we can get out of this the moment we realize who we are in reality. That is our immortal Self. That is the Truth. Truth is not far away from us. We are part and parcel of the Truth, *because we are eternal.* But not this body, not our personality is eternal. It will go. Our senses are not eternal, they will go. The real foundation of our being, our life, is eternal, is a life-force. But we do not know what life is any more than we know what electricity is, and yet we are using electricity all the time. So, the manifestation of electricity is an appearance, but the force itself is unknown and unknowable to us. It is unknown and unknowable to the ordinary mind. But when we have better knowledge, when we have realization of the source of all forces, then we know what it is. It is the expression of one force. The whole universe is living. There is no such thing as dead matter. But still we see it is dead matter, which is a delusion. You think that you are sick, you have a disease, an indigestion, or some kind of ache or pain. That is a delusion. You know, if you are spirit, you cannot have sickness. Spirit is never sick, and dead body is never sick. Then who is sick? If the dead body does not catch cold or have any indigestion, then where is the indigestion? That is a delusion. It is a kind of perplexing problem. But we have to go through it and transcend it.

APPENDIX B

HEART AND MIND

What is the underlying principle of the heart in contradistinction to the mind? The two terms, 'heart' and 'mind', are used in a very loose way in ordinary conversation. The heart refers to the feeling, and the mind includes a lot of other activities and other functions. According to the Vedânta philosophy, mind is not the same as the spirit, but it is the instrument of the spirit. In the Christian Science and in other New Thought, you will find the mind and the spirit, the soul and the life and eternal being all refer to the same thing. In psychology, you will find that the mind includes heart, feelings, emotion and everything. But when the word 'heart' is used, we call it *Chitta.* 'Blessed are the pure in heart, for they shall see God', says Jesus the Christ. There, the heart does not mean physical heart, but it refers to the feeling property of percepts and concepts; that is, after perceiving an object an impression is left in the mind. And all these impressions that we have gained must be purified. These impressions are the causes of future desires. If we wipe away these impressions that are stamped upon the mind substance, then the mind substance becomes pure. Then it gets the power of reflecting.

That idea is not given in any other philosophy except the Râja Yoga. The mind is regarded as the mirror, and if the mirror is covered with mud and dirt or dust, its reflecting power would be subdued. So, the mind of a worldly man or woman, who has all kinds of desires for the physical body and material world, has received all these impressions of material nature and they have formed like dirt or dust upon the mirror of the heart. These impressions will not die out unless they are forced out, but they will retain the germs of future desires. The future desires are the resultant of our impressions of previous experiences. As for instance, if you eat a new dish that is very delicious, after you have finished the particular act of eating, the impression of the taste will remain in the subconscious mind, and that impression will sooner or later create a desire for that kind of enjoyment of the same thing once more. And then, next time when you enjoy it, it will create another impression, and then the previous impression will be strengthened by the next impression So, every time you enjoy anything or experience anything, your subconscious mind is stamped, and that gets into a habit. *What we call 'habit' is but a series of impressions.* And it becomes so strong that it moulds our whole character and that is our second nature. The first nature was also produced in the same way. A person becomes a drunkard or a drug addict in the same way. But these impressions or *Samskâras* are the obstacles that are holding us down on this plane, and we cannot get the knowledge of the supreme Truth. To get this supreme knowledge we must purify our hearts. By the purification of the heart we mean that we should rub it off with discrimination. Instead of indulging in desires, some say, you should kill them out. But *you cannot kill them out.* There are certain cults that teach: 'Kill out all the desires and make your mind blank.' We cannot do that. It wil be absolutely impossible to do that. *We can reduce the number of desires by discrimination and not allowing indulgence. In that way we can purify our heart or mind.* So, the heart means the same thing as the mind, or feeling, or percept, or concept, which we have within us.

INDEX